GREAT BRITAIN

Text
Simona Tarchetti

Graphic design
Patrizia Balocco

Contents

2-3 One the most enchanting Scottish castles is in Glamis. This stately home, extensively renovated in the 17th century, belongs to the Earls of Strathmore, who are related to the Queen Mother.

4-5 The Palace of Westminster was completely rebuilt and redesigned in Gothic style by Barry and Pugin after the fire of 1834 and is situated along the left bank of the Thames. At the northern corner is the magnificent clock tower; well known symbol of London, it stands 318 feet high.

6 A lady of the English high society shows off her pretty hat at a race meeting.

7 Tower Bridge consists of two 216-foot-high towers and by a central part that can be raised to allow the passage of tall ships.

8-9 Only a part of northeastern Ireland belongs to the United Kingdom; it is a wide flat valley surrounded by old mountains which gently slope down to the sea.

10-11 In the smaller towns of Great Britain life passes quietly, far from the frantic rhythms of huge cities and the incessant noise of the factories in the industrialised areas.

12-13 "Trooping the Colour" is celebrated every year in June on the Queen's official birthday and on this occasion some regiments parade in honour of the sovereign.

14-15 The county of Surrey, to the southwest of London, contains many picturesque villages in woodland settings .

This edition published in 1994 by SMITHMARK Publishers Inc., 16 East 32nd Street, New York, NY 10016.

SMITHMARK books are available for bulk purchase for sales promotion and premium use. For details write or call the Manager of Special Sales, SMITHMARK Publishers InC., 16 East 32nd Street, New York, NY 10016; (212) 532-6600.

First published by Edizioni White Star.
Title of the original edition: Gran Bretagna un'isola al centro dell'Europa
© World copyright 1993 by Edizioni White Star. Via Candido Sassone 22/24,13100 Vercelli, Italy.

ISBN 0-8317-4064-7

Printed in Singapore by Tien Wah Press Color separations by Magenta, Lit. Con., Singapore.

Introduction

> . . . this little world,
> This precious stone set in the silver sea,
> Which serves it in the office of a wall,
> Or as a moat defensive to a house,
> Against the envy of less happier lands . .
> *William Shakespeare (Richard II)*

These words by England's national bard admirably describe the normally hidden but nonetheless deeply-felt attachment which the British have for their homeland. Despite a geologically enforced and politically desired separation from the European continent, Great Britain has made its influence felt in the whole world. Considered by historians to be the Mother of modern democracies, Britain has ruled over the destiny of many distant lands for a number of centuries. It still plays a leading role in the Commonwealth and the English language has become a lingua franca which is no longer limited to the fields of trade, politics and science. Even for simple cultural exchanges, so frequent among members of the European community and the peoples of the world, English is the most commonly used language. Although Great Britain is now considered to be a single political unit, three countries with different and quite distinct cultural backgrounds are represented in the glorious "Union Jack". The territory of the United Kingdom includes the countries of England, Wales, and Scotland, the province of Northern Ireland as well as a number of smaller islands off the British coast. The British people are proud of being British but they perhaps take even more pride in their separate cultural and linguistic traditions which are the heritage of their different ethnic origins.

Because of its position, isolated and sheltered at the same time by the North Sea on one side and the Atlantic Ocean on the other, the British archipelago has experienced long periods of isolation which allowed local populations to develop strong cultural traditions. The origin of these traditions dates back to the period in which the first occupants, after invading the island in successive waves, finally decided to settle there. Before

16 *The Cornwall peninsula becomes narrower as it stretches out between the Channel and the Atlantic Ocean. The region, which is extremely luxuriant because of the frequent rains, enjoys the best winter climate in the entire country.*

17 *The rooftop of a cottage in Clovelly, where steep, stone-flagged lanes are passable only by sheep and donkeys, and fishermen coming up from the port after a day at sea.*

18 top *Lincoln is a city of some historical importance and has a wonderful cathedral with three superb Gothic towers crowned by pinnacles.*

18 bottom *In Canterbury, Christ Church Cathedral, the most important church for Anglicans and the seat of the English primate, is a splendid example of English Gothic art.*

19 *The picturesque cathedral of St. Albans, a small town just outside London, is a wonderful structure in Romanesque-Norman style. Inside is kept the Ark of the Saint, the first English Christian martyr, to whom the church is dedicated.*

the most recent conquest of the island, by the Normans in 1066, the island was inhabited by Celtic tribes. These people kept livestock and they resisted the invading Romans for a long time. Gradually pushed northwards by successive invasions, they eventually found refuge in the north and the west and it is for this reason that Wales and Cornwall became and remain strongholds of Celtic language and custom. Indeed, the ancient religious rites of the Druids still form the basis of many feasts which are celebrated in our day and age. Many popular traditions in rural areas date back to pagan rites linked to the cult of nature and the cycle of the seasons which were the fundamental tenets of Celtic religion. The semantic structure of the English language originates from the Anglo-Saxon language, that is, from the language of the German tribes known as the Angles and the Saxons, who occupied the whole of England in the 5th and 6th centuries after the withdrawal of the Romans. Unlike the Roman invaders, they remained on the island, making a living from agriculture, which developed into a flourishing activity after wide areas in the Saxon counties of England had been cleared of trees. The growing stability of Roman and Anglo-Saxon settlements and the spread of Christianity stimulated the process of civilization and led to a refinement of arts and crafts and a progressive cultural enrichment. The epic poem which narrates the exploits of Beowulf and the religious poetry of Caedmon and Cynewulf are the prelude to the first works written in Old English. This language, which was polished in the course of the centuries, was then used not only for popular prose but was also in the splendid manuscripts produced in English monasteries of which many splendid examples can still be seen in the British Museum. Modern English originated from Anglo-Saxon and Gaelic and was also influenced by French which was the language of Norman conquerors, who, although of Nordic origin, had lived for over a century in France. The Norman Conquest also introduced new artistic trends. Norman churches and cathedrals had wide naves separated from the side aisles by columns and pillars which, rising in several series of arches, created a dizzying sense of height. Durham Cathedral is considered to be one of the oldest examples of that architectural style which in England is known as Norman and on the continent as Romanesque and its rib vaults are the first to appear in Northern Europe.

The solemn coronation of the Duke of Normandy as King of England at Westminster marked the end of foreign invasions and established the Abbey of Westminster as the coronation site of English sovereigns. The ethnic structure as it was defined in 1066 is the same as that which one finds in modern-day

England while the Scottish and the Welsh peoples are much more closely bound to their Celtic origins.

However, a country is not only the result of its historical and cultural past and its incessant efforts to create a modern society. People also choose where to settle and build their cities on the basis of the geographical lie of the land. The reason why cities were founded in certain areas while other areas remained agricultural is essentially due to geographical factors. Britain has a great variety of different landscapes: steep cliffs along the Atlantic coast, low-lying hills interspersed with woods and clear stretches of water in the Lake District, barren moors in the Scottish Highlands and arable land stretching almost to the coastline in Norfolk. The thing which all these various landscapes have in common is their verdancy, favoured both by the frequent rain-bringing depressions which originate over the Atlantic and by the mitigating effect of the Gulf Stream. While some areas of the British countryside have preserved their wild and unpolluted nature and provide shelter to a large number of animal species, the majority of the countryside bears the hallmark of man's presence. Generations of farmers have toiled to produce arable land and the changes brought about by the Industrial Revolution have radically changed the appearance of the landscape in the course of the last two centuries.

The ruins of textile mills in Lancashire and Yorkshire as well as the traces of old tin mines in Cornwall are popular sites for those tourists interested in "industrial archaeology". The smoke-stacks of steelworks in some towns in north-eastern England are an integral part of the national landscape. The process of rapid industrialization in the wake of the industrial revolution also radically modified the social structure of the country which up to that point had been organized according to essentially rural criteria. On the whole, the growth of large industrial cities was limited to the regions in which coal was mined and iron and steel produced. Elsewhere, city and countryside continued to live side by side. Not far from the major conurbations, seaports and industrialized regions of modern-day Britain there are many charming rural areas. This is the case of many villages in Northumberland and in the Valleys of the Ouse and the Trent. It is also true of Kent which is very close to London and is known as the Garden of England.

The towns which were built during the Industrial Revolution have a characteristic appearance. The centre is generally rather small and contains the older buildings and it is here that the majority of administrative and commercial activities are concentrated. This nucleus is surrounded by industrial

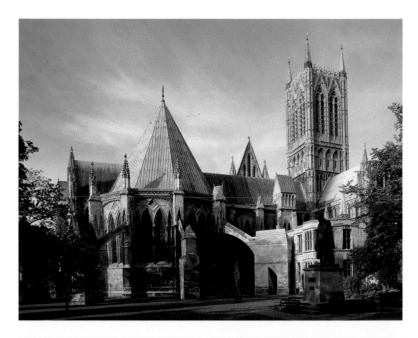

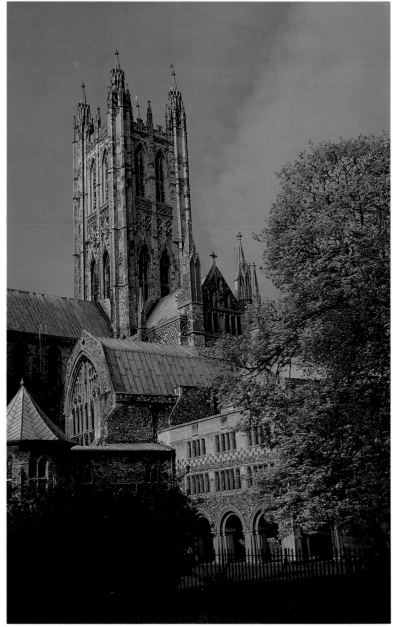

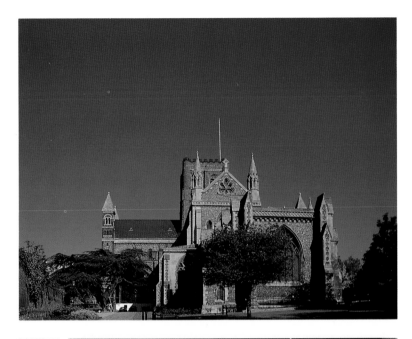

zones and by housing schemes consisting of rows of identical houses which were built for the workers towards the end of the last century. On the outskirts, like a halo, new residential zones containing many large public and private green areas have been constructed.

After World War Two a number of "New Towns" were built to house the over-spill populations of such large industrial cities as London and Glasgow. These towns were designed to provide all the social services and infrastructure necessary for modern urban life, while respecting the equilibrium between the inhabitants and the surrounding environment. The thing which most strikes one about Britain are the contrasts: the juxtaposition of old and new, built-up areas and untouched natural habitats, historical buildings which have become national symbols, and new, anonymous satellite towns on the outskirts of the larger cities. These contrasts are particularly sharp in London, which, especially in the wake of the increase in population brought about by immigration from Commonwealth countries, is the most cosmopolitan city in the world. The history of London really began during the Roman period when a bridge was built across the Thames and a settlement known as Londinium was founded. The city is built on a clay lowland on both banks of the Thames in a strategic point for maritime trade with Europe. From the ancient nucleus, called the "City," London gradually expanded as its commercial and financial importance grew. Mile after mile, Greater London incorporated all the surrounding villages including bucolic Hampton and Richmond and now has a surface area three times greater than that of Tokyo even though it "only" has nine million inhabitants. The metropolis is a disorderly agglomeration of districts, each with its own peculiar features and rhythms of life. The financial and commercial centre is still to be found in the City, a square mile of winding medieval streets towered over by skyscrapers and containing many beautiful ancient monuments as well as the majestic dome of St. Paul's. This is the masterpiece of Sir Christopher Wren, who was responsible for the rebuilding of this area after the terrible fire of 1666. Almost all the important historical monuments are situated in the old city centre and some of them were rebuilt after being destroyed or damaged during World War Two.

Some of London's most famous architectural masterpieces were built during the reign of Elizabeth I. Inigo Jones, who was a contemporary of Shakespeare, contributed to the embellishment of numerous royal palaces, aristocratic mansions, and public buildings. It was not until many centuries later, at the beginning of the 19th century, that the basis of the city's current appearance was laid. This was based on an innovative town plan by John Nash which encompassed the magnificent Regent Street, Piccadilly Circus, and the commemorative Trafalgar Square. The suburbs were left to their own devices and turned into grim dormitory settlements for the industrial working class. There are clear contrasts between areas of the city inhabited by those who continue their very typical "British way of life" and the districts in which the various ethnic minorities have settled.

The atmosphere which one breathes in Trafalgar Square or in Piccadilly Circus is a far cry from the smart, refined and exclusive atmosphere of the Gentlemen's clubs in Pall Mall. The elegant Georgian buildings in Mayfair and the houses in Belgravia with their white stuccoed columns are not very distant in geographical terms from the noisy streets of Soho lined with red-light cinemas and Chinese restaurants or from Knightsbridge, home to the thousand shining lights of Harrods, London's most famous and popular department store. Although many areas of London are full of bustling market-stalls, boutiques and international restaurants, there are also many quiet secluded areas and it is possible to seek refuge from the frantic pace of city life in one of the many pubs which are a little off the beaten track. As well as its many stately public buildings the centre of London also contains many gardens and parks where one can stop for a rest and a breath of fresh air. Some people think that London is too big, too noisy, and too expensive while others view it as a matchless cultural centre and a lively commercial market. One thing is certain: it is one of the most charming and inscrutable cities in the world.

London does not treat its river with the respect it deserves as source of the city's ever-growing prosperity from the period of Roman occupation until the middle of this century. However, in the Thames Valley the river once more plays a leading role in the creation of splendid landscapes and the banks of the Thames are dotted with many picturesque villages surrounded by green fields and woods. Oxford is also on the Thames and here the river flows past the spires and towers of the city. The chapel of Christ Church college is now the city's cathedral and every evening at 19:05 the 7 ton bell known as Great Tom, housed in Tom Tower, sounds out 101 strokes. Windsor Castle, one of the official residences of the Royal Family and the largest inhabited fortress in the world, is perched on a chalk hill overlooking the river. Aristocratic mansions, red-brick Tudor buildings and Norman abbeys suddenly appear around bends in the river, illuminated by the sun reflected on the smooth water.

The southern part of the country is

20 top *In addition to the famous observatory, Greenwich also houses the Royal Naval College, a prestigious school for naval specialization; since 1873 it has occupied the four major buildings of what was originally a hospital designed by Sir Christopher Wren.*

20 bottom *Near King's Lynn, an ancient town in Norfolk, is the Royal Palace of Sandringham, well known for its park that is frequently open to the public.*

characterised by green rolling hills which terminate on the coast as the white calcareous cliffs of Dover and Beachy Head. These were the first natural obstacles which invaders had to overcome in their attempt to conquer England. Not far from the coast lies the city of Canterbury which was a busy trading post during Roman times. St. Augustine of Canterbury founded a Benedictine monastery there and converted Aethelberht, fifth Jutish king of Kent and overlord of Britain. He later built a cathedral and Canterbury thus became established as the prime see of England, a position it has maintained ever since. The oldest parts of the present cathedral date back to 1070 but many new parts were added in the course of the following centuries. The most notable feature of the exterior is the Perpendicular central tower, built between 1495 and 1503 by Prior Thomas Goldstone. It is 235 feet high and is known as the Angel steeple from the gilded figure of an angel which formerly adorned the summit. At the west front it is flanked by towers whose massive tiered buttresses contrast the beautiful effect of the straight lines of the central tower. The cathedral is also renowned for its splendid stained-glass windows. Kent and Sussex contain many Anglo-Saxon and Norman remains and the landscape is embellished with many fortresses, castles, churches and cathedrals.

Brighton is a favourite holiday resort for Londoners who flock to its beaches in the summer. Here, one can also admire the splendid Royal Pavilion, a princely villa in Indian style built by Nash for the future King George IV. Tarred shacks where fishermen hang their nets to dry and small coastal markets which sell oysters and dried shark recall some of the descriptions in the novels of Charles Dickens.

Further to the west the landscape becomes more wooded and the cliffs along the coast are higher. This was the ancient Kingdom of Wessex and it was here, in a fictitious county called Wessex, that Thomas Hardy set some of his novels. Stonehenge, on Salisbury plain in Wiltshire, dates back to the late Neolithic and Early Bronze Age and is still surrounded in an aura of mystery. Corfe Castle, about 18 miles from Dorchester, has been in ruins since it was dismantled by Parliamentary forces in 1646. According to popular legend, this was the place where the Saxon king, Edward the Martyr, was murdered in 978. Winchester was the site of Celtic settlements as well as of the important Romano-British country town of Venta Belgarum. It also had links with King Arthur and the Knights and it later became the capital of the Kingdom of Wessex whose kings became the Kings of England. It was very prosperous after the conquest and its splendid Norman cathedral is the longest in England. Many

21 *During ebb tide, the "tongue" linking up the coastline to Saint Michael's Mount Isle can be explored on foot. On the island stands an old fortress, used over the centuries as a monastery, then again as a fortress, and now as a private residence.*

22-23 *Within the walls of the smart Pump Room in Bath – a lovely town with wonderful Georgian buildings – one can enjoy morning tea to a background of chamber music.*

archaeological remains in this southern part of the island bear witness to the fact that it has been inhabited continuously since pre-historic times.

The Celtic origins of the people of Cornwall are very pronounced and many traditions which have been jealously guarded and handed down from one generation to another are still kept alive in small fishing villages and busy market towns. Cornwall is a popular holiday destination for British and foreign tourists. Surfers skim over the waves at Newquay every summer and the golden beaches of Perranporth swarm with bathers, yachtsmen, amateur fishermen and holiday-makers attracted by the mildness of the climate. There are many coves along the Cornwall coastline which evoke images of secret caves and bands of smugglers in their struggle with the ubiquitous excise-man. Such stories are still told around the fires of some of the inns near the harbour at Falmouth. This was once the port of arrival for mail-ships coming from America and is still an important fishing village where skilled artisans build yachts and fishing boats. Plymouth, in the county of Devon, is a flourishing port and industrial centre and it was here that Drake played his most famous game of bowls. Sir Francis Drake was one of the founders of that Royal Navy which was destined to rule the waves and which was the instrument by which the British Crown extended its dominion over one quarter of the Earth's surface. However, in the southwestern part of England the real protagonist is the landscape. It can be desolate and bleak on the moors in Dartmoor National Park, quiet and romantic in the village of Polperro, charming on the long stretches of golden sand near Torquay, or rugged and barren at Land's End, the most western point in Great Britain, ceaselessly lashed by wind and waves.

The structure of the landscape is very different in East Anglia which consists of the counties of Norfolk and Suffolk. This fertile plain does not have a spectacular landscape, yet its rivers, canals and villages and trees inspired the works of such great landscape painters as John Constable and Thomas Gainsborough. There are gentle hills, marshlands, and lowlands crossed by a network of navigable canals. This region has always been isolated from the rest of England by thick woods and insalubrious marshes and the industrial revolution did very little to change the medieval appearance of many of its villages. Many of the cities in East Anglia are of historical and cultural importance. In the county of Norfolk there are at least 600 medieval churches and numerous stone towers built by the Saxons. Within the walls of Norwich there are a number of abbeys dating back to the period of religious persecutions. In fact, during the Middle Ages the victims of persecutions sought refuge in these marshy plains.

Cambridge is often mentioned along with Oxford as a prestigious university town, although there is a certain degree of competition between both cities. Cambridge University dates back to the 13th century and some of the world's most illustrious scientists have studied and worked here. This small, quiet country town possesses many wonderful architectural monuments and precious works of art. Visitors are astonished at the sight of the splendid stained glass windows of King's College Chapel which also contains Rubens' "The Adoration of the Magi". The city also boasts a replica of the Venetian Bridge of Sighs, albeit with a less mournful tradition. The Midlands, situated to the west of East Anglia, form a wide arc from the North Sea to the Irish Sea. They are the most industrialized and productive areas of Great Britain because of the presence of vast coal fields which were the source of that energy indispensable for the advent of the Industrial Revolution and for the economic development of the country. Unfortunately, this also produced many environmental problems and in fact, at one time, the landscape between Birmingham and Liverpool was often hidden by dark clouds of smoke billowing out from steel-mills and brickyards. Today, things have improved considerably and many of the coal mines have been shut down as alternative sources of energy have become available.

England's green and pleasant land can still be enjoyed to the full in the Cotswold Hills, which is the zone in which the Thames rises. Here, idyllic cottages built with local oolite glow with a warm golden colour and the sweet murmur of the water moving the paddle of an old mill provides the soundtrack to a bucolic calm. Nearby, at Stratford upon Avon, in the county of Warwickshire, one can attend a performance at the Royal Shakespeare Memorial Theatre which is built on the banks of the river Avon.

Wales is very different from the rest of Great Britain, and not only in a physical sense. This peninsula which stretches out into the Irish Sea is a true nation which is proud of its language and which jealously guards its age-old traditions. The history of this region is rich with tales of medieval heroes, furious battles, foreign invasions and desperate attempts at defense. The Welsh consider themselves as the only true Britons because their presence in the territory dates back to prehistoric times, as several prehistoric ceremonial stones and tombs dotted about the country can testify. Despite its early annexation to England in 1284 and the signing of the Act of Union in 1536 during the reign of the Tudors (who were of Welsh origin), the people of Wales have maintained their own distinct culture which

24 *In Rye, a once important medieval port on the Channel, nice houses and picturesque paved roads abound, evoking a heritage of hidden places from the time when the town was an important centre of smuggling and a shelter for sailors and pirates.*

25 top *In the county of Kent there are many old churches in picturesque settings.*

25 middle and bottom *The Thames, before it reaches London, flows past the rolling hills of Berkshire where quiet villages, meadows, and weeping willows line its banks..*

dates back to the pre-Christian kingdom created by the Celts in Britain. The landscape of Wales also has its own particular natural beauty. Green hills accompany the course of the rivers Wye and Severn, while, in the northwest, we encounter a bare mountainous landscape with paths winding between rocky outcrops and breathtakingly beautiful lakes in the Snowdon massif. In sharp contrast with this, slag heaps stand near the coal mines along the southern zone of the Black Mountains, the most industrialized and densely populated area in Wales. There are also the deep caverns in Dan-yr-Og with stalactites, stalagmites, and underground lakes and many other valleys which gently descend from the Welsh Marches towards England.

Like the landscape, the Welsh language also displays surprising features - now a cacophony of consonants, now a musical harmony of sounds. Welsh is a language built on past echoes, still alive in legends, in folk songs, and in ballads which are an integral part of Welsh social life. Music becomes a cultural expression when poets, dancers, and choristers come together at festivals called "eisteddfod" - where traditional costumes can be admired and Welsh friendly hospitality enjoyed. In Great Britain, most cultural contrasts and regional antagonisms arise not only because of a historical heritage of ethnic differences but also because of the rivalry existing between the values of the industrial society and those of the rural community. Economic activity, which led to an increase in the number of factories in Yorkshire and Lancashire during the Victorian Age, also highlights some of the differences between the North Country and the south.

The traditional industries of cotton and wool processing in Liverpool, Manchester, and Birmingham have been replaced, not without problems, by mechanical, chemical, pharmaceutical, and motor plants. The landscape in this region is rich in contrasts. On the outskirts of the industrial towns there are old spinning and weaving mills and these are interspersed with vast areas of natural beauty and fertile farming land. From Dovedale, a pretty valley where sheep dogs skilfully herd flocks, to the imposing rocky walls of the Pennines, where only the whistling of the wind and the loud noise of rivers disappearing over precipices can be heard, from the sandy beaches along the Northumberland coast to heather-covered moorlands, and the peat bogs of the Cheviot Hills on the Scottish border, the North Country offers a great quantity of interesting and fascinating views.

Historical events have left their traces in British towns; among York's principal attractions, in addition to the wonderful windows of its Minster, is a real treasure of Viking objects and hand-manufactured

25

items. The wonderful Durham cathedral with its elegant rib vaults is a precious example of the finest Norman architecture. Kendal, an lively town on the border of the Lake District National Park, is worth mentioning as a tourist resort that has been able to retain the quiet and genuine atmosphere typical of provincial life. The Lake District National Park in northwestern England is one of the English regions most frequented by Sunday tourists, holiday-makers, and keen naturalists. The landscape is undoubtedly one of breathtaking beauty; the dome-shaped mountains moulded by quaternary glaciers have produced a system of raised valleys and clearly defined upland plateaux.

The majestic expanses of water and the numerous "tarns" create romantic landscapes in which the blue sky blends with the mirror of the water's surface. The charming landscape reveals in the distance green hills furrowed by gushing torrents, steep slopes, and "practice" walls for experienced climbers - interspersed with meadows full of grazing herds. From this wonderful landscape many Romantic poets drew their inspiration; William Wordsworth created his verses on the shores of Esthwaite Water and experienced solitude in the Duddon valley, which is unknown to most tourists and therefore still unspoiled. Hadrian's Wall links Wallsend-on-Tyne with Bowness-on-Solway and was built as a frontier barrier under the Emperor Hadrian. It comprised a twenty-foot stone wall, ditches, turrets, "milecastles", fortresses and a double earthen mound or "Vallum". Impressive ruins are still visible at Chesters and Housesteads. This wall is the most important heritage left by the Roman Empire, or perhaps it is a monument to the determination with which the ancient tribes of the proud "Picts," the first inhabitants of Scotland, fought the legions of Julius Agricola. It was the Scots, however - Celts who spoke a Gaelic language and came from neighboring Ireland - who in the 12th century united Scotland in one single reign under Malcolm III. The capital city, Edinburgh, situated in the deep inlet of the Firth of Forth, is one of the most charming cities in Great Britain; its troubled historical events have worked upon the city structure, enriching it with remains and monuments as well as a precious artistic heritage. The elegant Georgian façades contrast with the austere beauty of the castle built on a rock dominating the whole city. The Royal Mile, which connects the castle with Holyrood House, is flanked by narrow lanes and "closes" and contains many 16th and 17th century buildings. The ancient capital went through a period of slow and progressive decay which began in 1707 when the Union Act was signed and the Scottish Parliament was subjected to that of Westminster. Holyrood House, the residence of the

26 One of the most popular English folk dances is the "Morris Dance," whose origins date back several centuries. Nowadays people still perform it dressed in traditional costumes.

27 On Edinburgh Castle esplanade a Military Tattoo is held during the Festival. This is a parade of military bands from all over the world — led, of course, by the Scottish detachment of "Pipes and Drums."

Monarch when she is in Edinburgh, has wonderful halls embellished with valuable Flemish tapestries. The former residence of Mary, Queen of Scots, this palace had been neglected for years until it regained its splendour during the last century, when receptions were held there on the occasion of King George IV's official visit. The Royal Family visits Scotland every year and spends a part of their summer holiday in Balmoral Castle, near Aberdeen, which is set in that wonderful scenery typical of the Scottish highlands.

Edinburgh turns into a huge and varied stage during the Edinburgh International Festival which takes place every summer. It is known all over the world and is rich in drama productions and musical events. For three weeks the city is an unparalleled cultural and artistic melting pot and every church and school hall becomes a venue for festival events. The festival coincides with the explosion of music and colours of the Military Tattoo which is held every evening on the Castle esplanade. Soldiers from all parts of the world participate in this spectacular event which is watched by spectators who are filled with alternating emotions; at one moment they are excited by the rousing rhythm of the military marches, at another they feel melancholy at the sweet sound of a Gaelic ballad.In Scotland the sense of identity - so strong in its traditions and the pride of its past - is as deeply rooted as anywhere else in the British Isles. From the first inhabitants, the mysterious Picts, to the Scots who succeeded in unifying the nation and keeping it independent until the beginning of the 18th century, Scottish history is full of clear references to the spirit of independence and to the efforts made to keep their singular but proud customs alive. The most evident cultural heritage of the clans, who built up the most important form of social organization among the mountain people of the cold highlands, is their characteristic tartans. An ample piece of woollen tartan cloth was originally wrapped around the hips in the traditional "kilt," and the remaining cloth, used as a plaid, covered the shoulders. The checked pattern and colours are distinctive for each single clan. The kilt is tightened at the waist by a belt from which the "sporran" hangs. This is a sort of leather bag, available in different shapes and colours, to be used on different occasions; it is indispensable, as it makes up for the lack of pockets in the kilt. This particular attire is completed by wool knee socks which are held up by hidden garters. A small dagger, known as a skean-dhu, is normally stuck in the right-hand sock. In addition to the colours of the kilt, each clan had its own tune, its official player, and of course, the typical bagpipes, another well-known symbol. This ancient musical instrument, used at all official events and popular feasts,

28 top *The stately Pembroke Castle overlooks a deep fjord of the western Welsh coast. Built in the 11th century and almost entirely restored two centuries later, it still retains the fierce lines of the Norman style.*

28 bottom *The old region of Cymru is very different from the neighbouring English countryside. It contains many castles and military fortresses whose wonderful towers are well known for their refined architectural style.*

29 top *The Tower of London is an imposing fortress originally erected to protect the city of London. The tower has been a palace, a prison, a place of execution and today it still houses the Crown Jewels.*

29 bottom *From the ruins of Urquhart Castle many visitors hope to see the profile of "Nessy," the legendary prehistoric monster, peeping out of the water of Loch Ness.*

30-31 *Along the shores of the wonderful Scottish lakes, surrounded by thick woods, the dark and disquieting shapes of castles dominate the pretty villages at their feet.*

consists of a leather bag and a series of pipes. The player blows air into the bag through the blowpipe and forces it out through sounding pipes. The chanter has a double reed and open holes through which the melody is played. Three drone pipes, closed at the ends and variously embossed, lean against the piper's shoulder. What elusive pride shines in the eyes of a Scotsman when the sound of the bagpipes is heard at the annual Highland Games! The qualities which clan chiefs looked for in their warriors, skill, strength and resistance, are still required in this competition in which tall, vigorous young men engage in a tug-of-war and the spectacular "tossing of the caber". The games are accompanied by Highland dancing competitions in which young boys and girls show their skills in the sword-dance and also by piping contests in which various bands compete for first prize.

Scottish tradition, folklore, and culture cannot be limited to the festivals of the capital or to the various Highland games which take place in many towns in the summer. Scotland offers the extraordinary beauty of its misty landscapes, the charm of its northern islands, the mysterious inhabitants of its lochs, and its castles - disquieting buildings set in the extensive Highland moors. Everywhere the appearance of the Highlands bears the clear traces left by the quaternary glaciers; the shores are deeply marked by numerous "firths"; the deep lakes, called "lochs," are long and narrow; the mountains have been shaped and greatly worn away by ice caps that covered the region in past eras. The high northwestern lands are among the most picturesque of Scottish areas. Beinn Eighe's mountains and woods alternate with the brackish marshes and dunes spread across the northern coast. The long lakes set in the hollow of Glen More give way to the wild expanses of Rannoch Moor, home only to waterfowl, eagles and deer. In the clear streams, trout and salmon abound.

The coastline is rocky and indented with many small islands. The steep and jagged cliffs pounded by the foaming waves give shelter to countless noisy colonies of seabirds nesting in cracks overlooking the sea which so generously nourishes them. Scotland's heritage of wildlife boasts many species, once spread all over Northern Europe and now living in only a few areas to escape destruction by man. Wild cats roam about in the pine and beech woods that form Scotland's vast forests, while the marten, with its long, sinuous body and yellow spot on its breast, is less common. Other typical animals of the region are Highland cattle, which show primitive morphological features traceable to the first hoofed mammals - long bristles to protect them from cold winds, long horns, and a relatively small stature are clear signs of their extreme hardiness; this animal is adapted to living on scanty pastures near steep mountains. These boundless spaces harbour wonderful and surprising discoveries, faithful proof of the unremitting work of natural forces only partially subdued by man. In the Grampians among the impressive high gorges and agricultural uplands, there are many superb castles, appearing as trembling outlines in the moonlight in the remote valleys - dark castles worth visiting for ancient memories and dreadful tales. Scotland is more than tartans or the sound of bagpipes, fascinating moors lashed by winds and the distant rumbling of a stormy sea. The Scottish people have a reputation for being thrifty, although they are friendly and generous with their guests. A true Scot enjoys a nice chat while he is sipping a pint of beer or eating a huge portion of hot "haggis," the famous national dish whose ingredients and preparation are secrets guarded with great care. The economic vitality of some cities has added one more feature to the country - the image of shipyards in the active city of Aberdeen, once a fishing port, now a modern base where foreign oil companies direct the drilling operations of off-shore rigs in the North Sea. The old processes of whisky manufacture are still the same in the Spey Valley distilleries, along with the memories of the tremendous fights for independence, the romantic sites described by Robert Burns, and even the aristocratic, exclusive greens of the Royal and Ancient Golf Club of St. Andrews, the most sophisticated golf club in the world. From the Hebrides, off the western coast of Scotland, the peaks of the Mountains of Antrim in Northern Ireland can be seen on clear days. Since ancient times the Irish Sea has not been an obstacle to exchanges between the Celtic and Christian cultures, but belongs to the two peoples collectively, both marked by historical and political events that arose from nationalistic and religious sentiments. The green landscape of Lough Neagh basin, which comprises most of Ulster's territory, is reminiscent of the pleasant expanses of the Scottish Highlands, while the folds and overthrusts in the structure of the mountains along the coast are also similar to those found in many parts of Scotland. The columns of basalt in the Giant's Causeway look like colossal steps going up to the green pastures from the sea.

Northern Ireland was officially created after the territorial division of Ireland in 1922, and is also known as Ulster. This was the name of an old Irish province consisting of nine counties, but, when the Republic of Ireland become independent from Great Britain, three of these (Donegal, Cavan and Monagham) became part of the new republic. It is difficult to establish with any precision the ethnic and cultural division between the two parts of Ireland. The inhabitants of the border

regions are all closely linked by commercial and family ties and it is also true that the true border line in some remote areas is not very precise since it corresponds to old borders which existed between these vast and scarcely inhabited counties in the 18th century. The two governments do not even agree on the length of the border: for the government of the South it is 278 miles long while the authorities in the North claim that it is 301 miles long. The clearest differences correspond to those visible signs of the heritage of hatred and sectarian violence which have influenced the life of the province for decades.

However, there are also historical, cultural and natural beauties. More than 300 million years of history are contained in the grottoes of Marbel Arch which extend underground in a series of chambers eroded in the calcareous rock. The 15th century Enniskillen Castle, in County Fermanagh contains a permanent exhibition of pre-historic finds from the area. As in all the other parts of the island, the territory of Ulster is dotted with crosses, gravestones and ruins of monasteries and churches. In many towns there are some charming period buildings and castles with Norman keeps. Belfast itself, despite its rapid industrial growth, has many beautiful examples of architecture.

The parliament meets in a splendid building in Palladian style built using the granite from the Mourne Mountains and Portland Stone. The Town Hall is also very imposing: a large renaissance construction planned at the beginning of the 19th century by Brumwell Thomas. Its copper domes now have a slight green tinge and in the interior one can admire the finishings in Italian marble and the splendid stained-glass windows. Despite the cultural and military barricades Belfast is a fascinating city and its inhabitants give tourists a warm welcome.

32-33 On Mainland, the largest of the Orkney islands, traces of prehistoric man are scattered everywhere. The photograph shows the "Stones of Stennes" which date from the Bronze Age.

A land of ancient traditions

" ... who piled these stones, and with the mossy sod
First covered o'er, and taught this aged tree,
Now wild, to bend its arms in circling shade,
I well remember. He was one who own'd
No common soul."

William Wordsworth

The historical wealth of Great Britain goes hand in hand with the vicissitudes of the various peoples who still maintain strong ties with their origins and traditions — those diverse cultural roots which clearly distinguish England, Scotland, Wales, and Northern Ireland. The island remains clearly divided in ethnic and linguistic minorities proceeding from those ancient Celtic populations who set themselves apart in Britain prior to the Roman invasion. Evidence of cultural separation is clearly seen across the territory. Wales, a Celtic stronghold, still today fiercely defends its own linguistic wealth. To the north, Scotsmen remain proud and attached to their particular customs, unchanged over time.

34 top *The Royal Pavilion, a unique building in the middle of Brighton, was rebuilt between 1815 and 1820 by the famous architect John Nash in the exotic style of Moghul palaces and Indian mosques.*

34 bottom *The eight imposing cylindrical towers of the castle, interconnected by walls up to sixteen feet thick, dominate the town and port of Conwy.*

35 *The unmistakable Clock Tower is one of the most famous symbols of London. Its great clock, familiarly known as Big Ben, strikes the hours of the day with proverbial punctuality, even though the mechanism must still be wound by hand.*

The metropolis of contrasts

36-37 *Sandwiched between the anonymous modern buildings and the skyscrapers of the city, St. Paul's Cathedral rises as a majestic building with classic lines conceived and realized by the great Sir Christopher Wren during the second half of the 17th century.*

38 *Located in the middle of London, Trafalgar Square is dedicated to to the memory of Admiral Nelson, whose defeat of Napoleon's navy at Trafalgar put an end to French plans to invade England. Behind the monument we can see the elegant façade of the National Gallery.*

39 *The lively intersection of Piccadilly Circus, frequently congested with traffic, is a typical meeting place for young Londoners and features many shop windows filled with the latest advertising myths.*

40 top *The British Museum was founded in 1753 after Sir Hans Sloane donated his large collection of books and antiquities to the Nation. It is one of the largest museums in the world and contains tresures from all parts of the world.*

40 right *Buckingham Palace was built at the beginning of the 18th century as the private residence of the Duke of Buckingham. It was rebuilt by King George III and since then has been the official London residence of the Sovereign.*

40 bottom *Many tourists still expect to see London's famous red telephone boxes, but these have now been replaced by more modern and functional public telephones.*

41 *Tower Bridge, built between 1886 and 1894, was desigend by H. Jones and J.W. Barry.*

42-43 *Many of the most important government offices are to be found in Whitehall, a wide boulevard stretching from Trafalgar Square to the Houses of Parliament.*

Westminster Abbey is the place where the British Sovereigns are crowned. It is also the burial site of many kings, queens, dignitaries, poets, and writers. The present appearance is the result of an architectural renovation of an ancient Saxon church. The Gothic building, which inspired some of the great French cathedrals, was begun around the mid-13th century. The two towers were added by Christopher Wren in the 18th century. The vast interior is divided into three naves adorned by many monuments and funerary sculptures. The coronation throne, made of oak, is located behind the main altar and has the "Stone of Scone," the ancient throne of the Scottish sovereigns, mounted in its base.

The cities and their history

46 *Edinburgh, Scotland's capital, is one of the most beautiful towns in Europe. The main street, Princes Street, runs from east to west with shops, hotels, and department stores, as if someone had drawn a boundary between the modern buildings of the capital and the wide, green expanses that reach Edinburgh Castle at the foot of the hill.*

47 top *From a small Gallo-Norman village, Belfast became a great business and industrial centre thanks to the rich deposits of iron and coal found in the area.*

47 bottom *Birmingham presents a modern aspect notwithstanding its ancient origins. It is the second largest town in Great Britain in terms of population density and economic importance.*

48 *The city of York is dominated by England's largest cathedral, York Minster. This is a wonderful example of the evolution of the Gothic style in England. Its façade with splendid stained glass windows is flanked by two towers built in the 14th and 15th centuries in the so called Perpendicular style.*

49 top left *Hometown of the Beatles, seat of two important soccer teams, Liverpool is an active business and industrial city and the second busiest United Kingdom port for overseas traffic.*

49 top right *The lively town of Leeds in West Yorkshire has gradually evolved into a modern manufacturing centre.*

49 bottom *Glasgow is built on the river Clyde and its economic rise in the 19th century was principally based on ship building and commerce. The city is now the home of Scottish Opera and ballet and contains many architectural monuments and excellent art collections.*

Traces from the mists of time

50-51 *From the Neolithic period, a great inexplicable megalithic complex challenges the slow and unrelenting passage of time. Stonehenge still carries within its stones the essence of its primitive function, leaving room only for legends and the varied interpretations of archaeologists and astronomers.*

51 top *The interesting discovery of Skara Brae in the Orkney Islands includes an entire prehistoric village dating back more than 4,000 years and very well preserved.*

50 top *Hadrian's Wall was built to protect the fertile and civilized southern regions under Roman domination from the belligerent Scots. Indelible traces can still be found of the 80 miles of the great wall and of the 12 forts spread along its entire length.*

The admirable achievements of man

Beautiful cathedrals stretch towards the heavens with their towers and pinnacles soaring over the surrounding rooftops in all parts of England, from the countryside of Kent to the industrial regions of the north. Cathedrals built in the Gothic style began to replace their Norman predecessors from the 13th century onwards. Ely Cathedral, built on the foundations of a Benedictine monastary, has a splendid octagon and Lady Chapel built in the Decorated style. The introduction of pointed arches meant the downward thrust of the weight of their own material and of that above was converted into outward thrusts resisted by buttresses. For this reason walls cound be thinner and even partially replaced by windows such as the rosettes which can be seen in many Gothic cathedrals. Thus cathedrals could be built higher and were much more luminous inside. the fan vaults of Wells cathedral constitute a remarkable example of this architectural style. The star vaults of Salisbury cathedral (1220-1266) are typical of the so-called Early English style.

52 left *Wells is a city in Somerset on the southern flank of the Mendip Hills and its mighty cathedral was built between the 12th and the 14th centuries. Its fan vaults are an outstanding example of Gothic architecture and they are enriched with decorative elements in the shape of upturned arches.*

52 right *The lovely cathedral of Ely, built on the ruins of a 7th-century Benedictine monastery, was completed in 1351. Its central nave is surmounted by a marvellous octagonal skylight, made of wood and glass.*

The delightful town of Bath, the renowned thermal spa, is known for its architecture and festivals, for its beautiful shops and excellent tourist facilities. The Romans were the first to build a great thermal complex in their ancient "Aquae Sulis" to exploit the local hot water springs, but not until the 17th century did Bath enjoy an exceptional development from the exploitation of the thermal phenomenon, thus becoming a destination for those who wished to "take the waters". During its expansion the little town was designed by architect John Wood, who, leaving a unique urbanistic imprint, conceived the rectangular space of Queen Square, the circular "square" of the Royal Circus surronded by neoclassic buildings, and the elegant complex of the Royal Crescent within a scenic Georgian structure that encloses a vast park.

54 *In the background is the beautiful cathedral of Bath. It dates back to 1499 and is a typical example of the so-called Perpendicular style. In the foreground is a part of the Roman Baths which made use of the springs of hot water found on this site.*

55 *Pulteney Bridge, on the river Avon, is the only work completed by Robert Adam at Bath and was built between 1769 and 1774. A particular worthy of note is the houses built on the bridge from which one has a splendid view of Parade Gardens.*

56-57 *A splendid image of the interior of the Beauchamp Chapel in the Parish Church of St. Mary's in Warwick. This chapel, built in the 15th century, is in the Perpendicular style and contains the tombs of the Counts of Warwick.*

58-59 *A short distance outside Nottingham, on the road to Derby, lies Wollaton Hall, a splendid Elizabethian residence set in a large park.*

Fairytale castles

60-61 Windsor Castle, a royal residence since its construction, is the largest occupied building in the world. It stands near London on a rocky hill and dominates the right bank of the river Thames. The building is surrounded by a beautiful park of nearly 2,000 hectares, where members of the Royal Family often enjoy riding. The architectural structure has been repeatedly enlarged over the centuries and includes an elegant Norman circular tower, the Horseshoe Cloister (an original, horseshoe-shaped cloister built in 1480), and the sumptuous royal apartments. St. George's Chapel, divided into three naves, is made precious by the beautifully carved wooden choir and by the standards of the knightly Order of the Garter.

62-63 On the wild Scottish moors, in the wooded hills or on the shores of the many lochs, the visitor often comes across a castle. Many of these have now been converted into guest houses or hotels but they still maintain their charm. The picture shows Eilean Donan Castle on the shores of Loch Duich.

An enterprising people

"At the station I became a modern Englishman, enthusiastically proud of modern England's science and energy . . . That station, with its thousands of trains dashing off in all directions or arriving from all quarters, was sufficient to elate me!

Wonderful evidences of English skill and enterprise . . . chimneys high as cathedral spires, vomiting forth smoke, furnaces emitting flames and lava, and the sound of those gigantic hammers, wielded by steam . . . "

George Borrow

The post-war economic boom and the immigration from Commonwealth countries brought many different ethnic groups to Britain and this led to the creation of a cosmopolitan society in many British cities. For many British people, going out for a meal involves a visit to the local Chinese or Indian restaurant and if one has forgotten to buy something for the supper, one just pops down to the local store which stays open until late in the evenings and is often owned by an Indian or a Pakistani. The differences between the English, Scots, Irish and Welsh are less evident to the visitor but each of these groups has their own particular accent and customs. On the whole, all these groups live in harmony because of the traditional British respect for the privacy and personal freedom of others.

64 top *A young boy wearing the typical bowler hat which is sold to foreign tourists much in the same way as they are offered gondolier's hats in Venice.*

64 bottom *"Say cheese, please", a typical image of a family from the rural parts of Scotland or Ireland.*

65 *The pinstripe suit, bowler hat, and umbrella – this is the look of the typical English gentleman.*

The workshop of the mind

Schooling is very important for the British. Besides "educating our masters" as a politician claimed in the late 19th century after the vote had been given to the majority of the male population, it also encourages socialisation and sporting endeavour. So-called "Public schools" are really exclusive and expensive private schools where many parents make economic sacrifices to send their offspring in the belief that a good

66 top While the university is in session, the streets of the city throng with students from the various colleges, the oldest of which is University College, founded in 1249.

66 right The Great Court of Trinity College is the large and beautiful courtyard of Cambridge's most famous college. Trinity College was founded by Henry VIII in 1546 and its library, built by Wren between 1676 and 1685, is admired every year by thousands of tourists.

education is the passport to success. Certain schools such as Eton, have a glorious tradition and, even today, the schoolchildren still wear top hats and tails and they did in the days of "Tom Brown's Schooldays". The two oldest universities of Oxford and Cambridge were once very elitist, but this has become slightly less so since the end of World War Two. However, they are still very attached to their traditions of academic and sporting excellence and there is intense rivalry between the various colleges. An Oxbridge education was once considered essential to make a career in the Civil Service. The more modern universities are often referred to as "Red-brick universities".

67 The origin of Oxford University dates back to 1163 when some teachers and students left Paris University and chose this city as their new seat. The first large college buildings were constructed in the 13th century and since then, the reputation of Oxford as a centre of learning has continued to grow.

68-69 The imposing Cathedral of Canterbury, founded in A.D. 602 by St. Augustine, towers over the medieval streets of the city. The cathedral is a haromonious ensemble of different styles; the central nave was built around 1400, while Bell Harry Tower is one hundred years younger.

Cool lawns
within the town

Love for nature and animals is one of the most outstanding features of the British character. The country boasts many protected areas and natural parks but, particularly in the great cities, ample space is reserved for public greens so that each citizen can enjoy a well deserved rest in the shade of ageless trees, or a romantic walk through flowered fields. Even London, notwithstanding the enormous building expansion, has never neglected or reduced its beautiful parks.

70 top Wollaton Hall, near Nottingham, is set in a beautiful park containing red and roe deer.

70 bottom Hyde Park extends for 394 acres in the heart of London. Especially in summer the park is a popular destination of Londoners and tourists who can have a walk in the shade of its magnificent trees or hire a deck-chair for a moment of relaxation.

71 Windsor Great Park contains magnificent gardens with over 25,000 species of plant, including one of the largest collections of rhododendron in the world.

72-73 Windsor Park also contains a well equipped riding school where one can hire a horse and go for a ride.

From the land to the man, from the man to the land

Great Britain's rural areas enjoy profit from agricultural activities and cattle breeding. Thanks to the climate's high humidity, fields and pastures abound. The hardiest races of sheep thrive on the more forbidding uplands and the Yorkshire moors, while the more valuable sheep flourish on the luxuriant meadows of Kent, Sussex, and the Midlands.

74 *A sheep market in an agricultural town in East Sussex. There many flocks of sheep on the lush southern downs and they produce high quality wool.*

75 *Sheep are left free to graze all year round on the Welsh hills. They are only herded together for dipping and for shearing.*

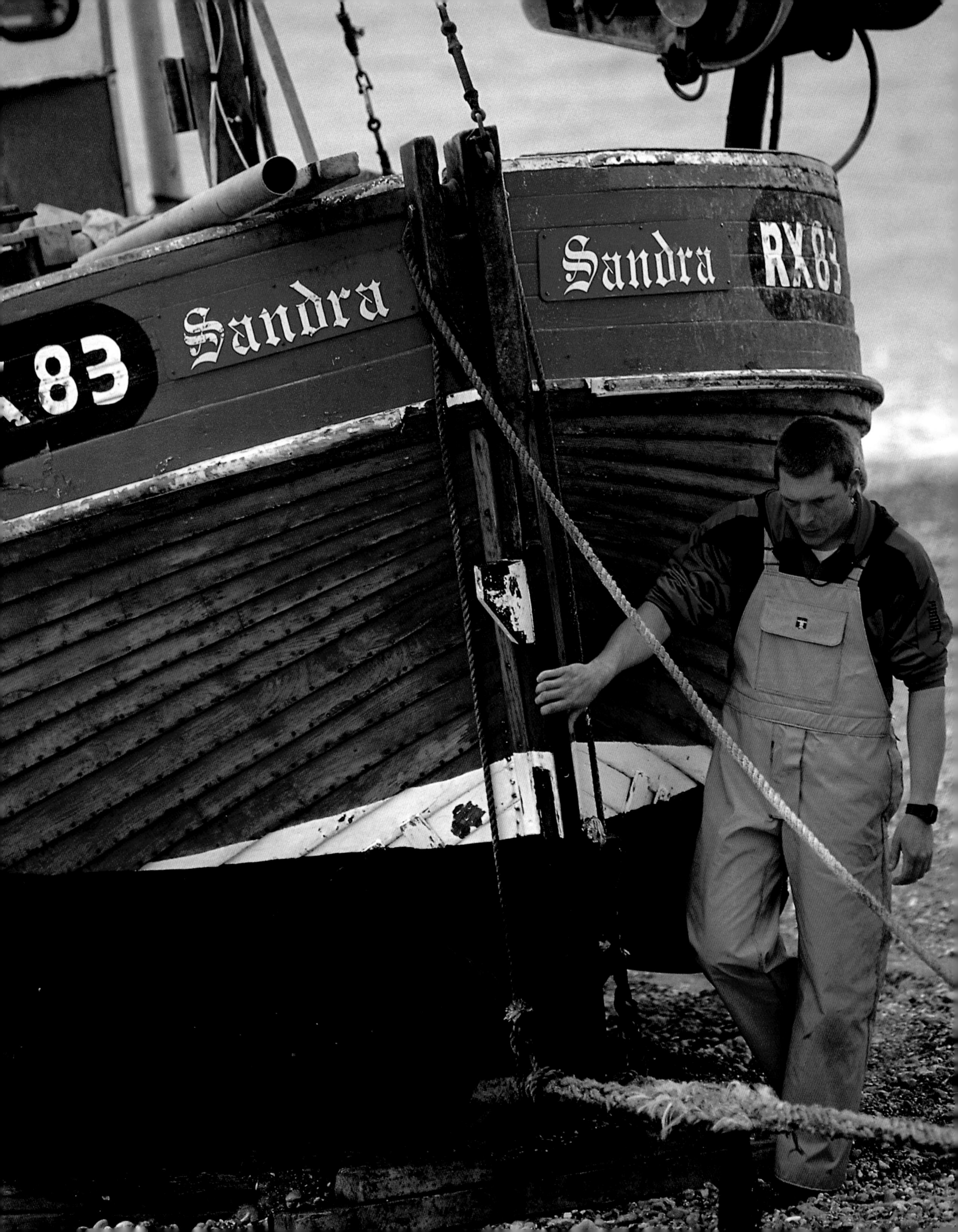
83
Sandra
Sandra
RX83

A daily challenge

Fishermen's work is difficult. Often the sea is dangerous and exhausting, and getting the fish aboard is not enough to make one forget weariness and loss of sleep. At the port's docks, particularly in the small centres of east Sussex along the coast and away from the great, noisy shipyards, loving artisans build fishing trawlers piece by piece using only strong, honest, seasoned timber.

A unique corner of London

Until recently London's biggest fruit, flower and vegetable market, Covent Garden is now a meeting place for musicians and travelling artists who give impromptu open-air concerts. The site of the market has been converted into a new shopping and entertainment development which contains many boutiques, restaurants

and cafes. Covent Garden was London's first square and was built in the Italian Style by Inigo Jones in the 1630's. The church still survives although the square has been rebuilt. It was originally conceived as one composition, the houses having uniform facades with arcaded ground floors and giant plasters above. From the amateur music of the rock and punk bands in the square one can move to the nearby Opera House, where one can hear some of the world's best artists. If one is not interested in opera, one can spend a quiet evening chatting in Tutton's Cafe or in one of the many pubs to be found in this area.

Evenings in good company

80-81 *The kilt was originally the dress of highland clansmen and was a rather simple garment. In the last century, Sir Walter Scott persuaded King George IV to wear a kilt on his visit to Scotland, and since then a very elaborate pleated kilt has been worn by soldiers in Scottish regiments and by pipers and drummers of pipe bands. Very few Scotsmen actually wear the kilt on a day to day basis and it is more likely to be seen at weddings or at such events as Highlands Games when even the members of the Royal Family appear dressed in tartan.*

81 *Pub entrances are usually discreet and dimly lit.*

A lively tradition of sport

84-85 *Sport is very important in Great Britain and many modern sports were first invented here. Rugby was invented at Rugby School and golf is said to originate from Scotland. Soccer is certainly the most popular spectator sport although cricket is also extremely popular in some counties of England and has been exported to many former British colonies.*

86-87 *Some people seek their moments of relaxation in a small sailing boat.*

88-89 *A long ocean wave dies on the beach in a ripple of foam.*

Top hats and pretty hats

Royal Ascot is more than an exciting race meeting where thoroughbred horses race for prestigious prizes. It is also one of the high points in the English social calendar and the ladies who are permitted into the Royal Enclosure vye with each other to show off the most extravagant hats. For the gentlemen, top hats and tails is de rigeur.

Time-honored traditions

Commemorative celebrations connected with the monarchic tradition still offer an irresistible attraction for the British people. It is always a copious and festive crowd that attends the great "Trooping the Colour," (shown here) the splendid military parade of Her Majesty's Regiments, who march on the Horse Guard esplanade in a feast of dress uniforms including shining horse-tail helmets and polychrome flags and banners.

94-95 A regiment of Guards wearing their characteristic headgear, normally have a homely and welcoming atmosphere.

96-97 Even pastimes such as hunting and fishing are traditional sports and unmistakable indications of a certain lifestyle typical of English aristocracy.

93

Many centuries ago, each clan chief in the Highlands chose the strongest warriors at the end of hard competitions during which young Scots had to pass tests of skill and strength. Some of the particular aspects of this ancient local culture are manifested in the Highlands Games, athletic and non-athletic competitions which take place in summer in various parts of the region. During these games, young people show off in skilled dances, exciting ritual combats, competitions of agility and of physical strength, and in choirs exalting the Scottish land and people, accompanied by the sound of bagpipes. The most famous of these events takes place at Braemar, attended by the Royal Family as guests of honour coming from their summer residence at nearby Balmoral Castle.

The villages and
the countryside

"The whole terra firma . . . makes the isle
of Britain seem to be one solid rock,
as if it was formed by Nature to resist the
otherwise irresistible power of the ocean."

Daniel Defoe

Great Britain's landscape is marked by
an incredible variety of scenery,
shaped by the slow changing of the
seasons and by the unrelenting
actions of man. Green is the
dominant colour – in the thousand
shades of the cultivated fields, in the
woods and in the peat bogs. In
contrast are the chromatic variations
of the sky – clear and blue sea or
leaden and dismal when rains and
storms come from the west and the
ocean swells threateningly. The
coasts, now steep, now hospitable,
withstand the lashing winds and offer
safe shelter to the British people, who
have always defended with great
strength that separation from the
continent that today is synonymous
with freedom and national identity.

100 *Many of the seaside resorts on the
Sussex coast are immersed in a
luxuriant greenery.*

101 *Beachy Head cliff, striking in its
wild beauty, rises more than 557 feet
above sea level.*

The contours
of the island

102-103 *The white cliffs of Dover can be seen in the distance as one approaches Great Britain during the Channel crossing. These steep banks, made by marine deposits dating back to the Cretaceous age, gave the country the ancient name of Albion, after the colour of the rocky formations raised above the sea by tectonic movements. The island's evocative calcareous cliffs form a raised edge along the whole southeastern coast and have been a natural protection against many invaders.*

104-105 *Atlantic Ocean waves break unceasingly on Land's End, the windy and bare headland at the extreme western point of England.*

105 top *Sandy beaches, warm, inviting climate, and flowering Sussex gardens contribute to the enhanced appeal to tourists of the seaside resorts of this part of England.*

105 middle *High and indented, or sandy and wind-sheltered, the Walsh coastline reveals interesting natural scenery where fauna and flora are protected in national parks and reserves.*

105 bottom *To the north of the estuary of the river Humber are charming seaside resorts with steep cliffs and tranquil sandy coves.*

106-107 *Rocky promontories and beautiful beaches along the western coast of Devon enclose romantic small fishing villages.*

105

108 left *After a long hard day at sea, their boats moored in the ports, ishermen unload the fruits of their labour onto the pier – sole, red mullet, cod, and even oysters and crabs.*

108-109 *Whitby, home town of the explorer James Cook, is an ancient port surrounded by picturesque fishermen's cottages. During the day, nets are mended along the steep alleys of this lovely seaside resort.*

110-111 *The Kent coast has a well deserved reputation for sunny beaches and lush countryside.*

Postcard from the charming countryside

Great Britain preserves splendid natural landscapes which, thanks to the perennial ecological sensitivity of the Anglo-Saxons, are adequately and far-sightedly protected. The most intact lands of the island date back to the first half of the 19th century, when a few brave and keen naturalists privately purchased the territories with the exclusive intent of rescuing them from the devastating action of the growing industrial civilization. In fact, with the development of building activities, the mining exploitation, and the widespread use of chemical products in agriculture, many delicate balances between fauna and flora were upset. In 1949, with the establishment of the Nature Conservancy, the British government began to create national reserves for the protection and conservation of natural scenery.

112 *Green pastures for sheep and abundant water are special features of Warwickshire, in the Heart of England.*

113 top *In the distance are the imposing mountains of Snowdonia National Park.*

113 bottom *The Lake District contains within itself all the beauty and majesty of nature.*

114 *The presence of various locks along the upper reaches of the Thames make it navigable and boats or barges are available for hire should one wish to pass a few days in this pleasurable manner.*

The yellow flower of rape, which is grown for rape-seed oil, contrasts with the green woodlands inhabited by foxes and pheasants and other wildlife.

GAMSWORTH OLD HALL
Rebuilt by Sir THOMAS FITTON Knt MCCCCLXXII.
Restored by RAYMOND and MONICA RICHARDS MCMLI.

The charming provinces

Small villages in idyllic rural settings
are still the true heart of the nation.
Few of them are very well known
but they are closely linked to the
people's ancestral traditions. The
work and toil of generations of
farmers who felled woods and
drained marshes led to the creation
of the first villages and hamlets,
which were built with local stone

and were in perfect harmony with
the surrounding landscape. Isolated
hamlets are dotted among the steep
hills of Cumbria while small cottages
built of golden sandstone nestle by
sunny creeks in Dorset. Of particular
interest to visitors are the
characteristic signs hanging outside
boarding houses which offer
accommodation for the night. In the
smaller towns the inns preserve a
sort of ancient charm and their
names recall famous people,
illustrious citizens or, more simple,
animals and scenery.

116-117 top *The county town of Chester was originally a Roman fortified settlement and the very name is derived from the Roman "ceaster" (a Roman fort). The characteristic "Rows" are medieval houses with shops in the arcades of the bottom two floors.*

117 bottom *Typical pub signs photographed in Stratford-upon-Avon.*

HARLEQUIN

FANCY DRESS HIRE 225915

Masks, Wigs
Stage Make-up
Hats

Ladies Evening
Dress Hire
Period Clothes

"Shopping" is an English term currently used in other countries, where it takes a precise and slightly restrictive meaning. In Great Britain this word does not only mean to make purchases, but it entails the delightful art of being able to evaluate the most appealing product among all the goods displayed in the window. London is traditionally the shopping capital; here choices range from department stores to small specialty shops, from high-fashion boutiques to secondhand markets. It is enough to know how to choose the area to suit requirements and finances, from the exclusive Bond Street to the many departments of Harrods, from the rather commercialised Carnaby Street to the colourful stalls of Portobello. Each day sees the celebration of that ageless dilemma which is a vital part of the London metropolis – of the contrast between past and future, between clothing befitting tradition and social position and clothing mass produced and made to measure. However, Great Britain offers fantastic shopping opportunities, and the wise tourist will be able to discover – in every little window and in each provincial market – the most characteristic goods of the place: pretty Nottinghamshire lace and refined Devon glassware, fine Staffordshire china, soft woollen items in Lancashire and Yorkshire, and plaid cloths in Scotland.

120-121 *Among the gentle hills of the English countryside are hidden graceful villages with stone cottages shining in the golden sunlight, with well tended gardens and pretty balconies filled with pots of variegated flowers.*

Distant archipelagos

122 *The Orkneys are a group of 67 islands located north of Scotland; lashed by storms and north winds, the smaller islands are often inhabited only by sea birds and seals.*

123 *The croft, a typical farm of the northern islands, supplies cereals, vegetables, and peat to the fishermen who fish for cod, mackerel, and herring.*

A rich and lively land

124 *In the Peak District extensive water basins are imprisoned by the rocks that delineate the northernmost area of the park, named Dark Peak because of its peculiar red sandstone. A varied flora grows on the calcareous plateaus, rich in rare botanical species whose habitat is often associated with extensive ash woods.*

125 *The mountains of Wales, high altitude lakes, and the very green hills at the foot of the mountains of Snowdonia National Park constitute wonderful natural scenery that attracts keen sportsmen, fishermen, climbers, tourists, and other visitors from every part of the country who are fascinated by the beautiful valleys and moors.*

126-127 *Yet more wonderful pictures of the British landscape – clear water expanses are common in the Lake District, the most romantic and fascinating region of the island; here nature has inspired many poets with feelings of beauty and admiration but also of dark solitude in the face of such awesome silence.*

Photo credits: